Nicki Minaj: The Pink Book

An Unauthorized Biography of Nicki Minaj

Written by

Valerie Mitchell

* * *

Illustration by
Samuel Redfield

ISBN: 150775986X
ISBN-13: 9781507759868

DEDICATED TO MAY.

CHAPTER ONE
The Early Years

If you could turn back the hands of time, to December 8, 1982, and head on over to St. James, a district of Port of Spain, in Trinidad and Tobago, you would be very near a newborn Onika Tanya Maraj, born to Carol and Robert (some sources have his first name listed as Omar) Maraj. Robert is mixed with Afro and Indo-Trinidadian, while Nicki's mother, Carol, is Afro-Trinidadian. Little did anyone know, that young Onika would one day become a megastar known to the world as Nicki Minaj. At only three years old, Nicki and her older brother stayed with their grandmother, as their mother looked for a new home in New York, NY. This move was prompted by her father, Robert, abusing alcohol and drugs, and trying to kill her mother by burning down their home.

"A lot of times, when you're from the islands, your parents leave and then send for you because it's easier when they have established themselves; when they have a place to stay, when

they have a job. I thought it was gonna be for a few days, it turned into two years without my mother".

In a July of 2012 interview, Nicki's mother, Carol Maraj, would tell Trinidad & Tobago Express' Renee Cummings this:

"My strength came from my children, my hope, and my reason for living..."

"I couldn't give up. They kept me going. I decided enough was enough. I'm leaving and I'm not going back. I had to take care of me and live for me. But it took a long time before I reached to that place."

The tenth of eleven children, Carol Maraj grew up in St. James, and grew up with her own familial issues:

"When I was in high school, one day I came home and my 18-
yearold brother was breaking up all the louvers in the
windows," Maraj said. "He was destroying everything. There
was a lot of trauma in the house...There was just a lot of trauma
in my early teens because of his illness. I was often afraid for
my life."

* * *

At the age of 20, she got married.

She worked several jobs, including as an Accounting Clerk at the National Insurance Board and as a foreign exchange teller at the National Commercial Bank.

"If I only looked at someone it was an argument..."

"If we went out, I couldn't dance with anyone. If someone who knew me saw me out in the street and I spoke to that person, it was a big argument and curse out in the street. I didn't realized it then, those early signs of abuse. I was very young when the abuse started."

She told Renee Cummings that her dad had filed for her Green Card for her.

At the age of 24, Carol Maraj moved to the Bronx, enrolling at Munroe College. 6 months later, Omar arrived, as Carol wanted to keep the family together. Omar had gotten a job at American Express.

"At first, it was nice, very nice..."

"He was cooking for me and doing a lot of nice things."

"The children came a few years after..."

Nicki and her brother stayed in St. James for several

years, with their grandmother, Carol's mother.

"They were in very good hands. My mom took good care of them."

Carol said that her father helped her to purchase her first house on 147th Street, off of the famed Rockaway Blvd., in Queens, NY.

Unfortunately, Nicki's father, Robert, like many other men and women in the mid 80's, fell victim to the rising crack epidemic, which hit New York City like a tidal wave.

"There was a lot happening in that house...I didn't know my husband was a crack addict. But one winter night, in December 1987, he went into a rage, he was demanding money, he was so angry, and I didn't have any money."

Reflecting on the situation, Carol said:

"When did all of this happen? How did all of this happen? I was a 27-year-old woman, working hard, trying to be happy in my own way and then this devastation just comes upon me," she said. "The neighbors are hearing. You have to hide your face and bend your head. God didn't make me for this. I kept telling myself God didn't make you for this. God didn't create you for this. I promised myself I wasn't going to give up until I made me right. When things fell apart I always looked for another door because I knew this

wasn't in God's plan for me. I never stopped going to church. Even if my eyes were blood-shot red I was in church. I had to refill on God's grace because my life had run dry."

Nicki Minaj would go on to later say

She describes Robert's upbringing, shedding light on the fact that his life wasn't a walk in the park either.

"His dad passed away when he was 14," she said. He had a lot of responsibilities because he had to care for five siblings. His mother put a lot of pressure on him and he was beaten for everything."

Nicki Minaj, in an interview with Simon Hattenstone for The Guardian, would go on to say this, in regards to her father:

"It's weird, because when he was on crack, he was more peaceful, and when he would drink, he became loud and violent. Each drug has its own spirit. You could see it on the person and feel it in the room."

Carol told Renee Cummings that her and Robert are now separated.

"A few years ago, he said he changed, and he

wanted help. I still love him. But as a brother in Christ. We've been over for more than 10 years now."

When she was five years old, Nicki moved to the United States, in an area that would become legendary within the Hip Hop culture that Nicki herself would use to catapult to fame: South Jamaica, Queens, New York City.

"I thought it was gonna be like a castle, like white picket fence, like a fairy tale. I got off the plane and it was cold. I remember the smell... I had never seen snow... I remember the house. I remember that the furniture wasn't put down. It was, like, piled up on each other, and I didn't understand why, 'cause I thought it was gonna look like a big castle."

Nicki attended P.S. 45 (Clarence Witherspoon School), before going to Elizabeth Blackwell Middle School 210 in Queens, New York. It was during this era in Nicki's life where she played the clarinet.

"I started hearing a lot of arguing, and I didn't know why, I was always very nervous, very afraid. So I knew that wasn't normal. My father would yell and curse a lot... It was right in the crack era. We didn't know, but he fell victim to crack shortly after he moved to America... When you're on crack, you can't keep a job . And when you can't keep a job, you don't have money. And when you don't have money, you steal. And you

steal from your family."

As her father would turn to drugs, it seems as if young Nicki turned to something else to get away from the world that had been created for her. To escape from her harsh reality, and in hindsight, perhaps a bit of foreshadowing in the overall story of her life, young Onika began role playing and speaking in different voices. Perhaps having an inner desire to help others, and possibly inspired by her mother, who worked as a nurse's aid, Nicki would oftentimes pretend to be either a teacher or a nurse, eventually even declaring that she would become a nurse, in a video that would surface years later and become viral, as the young woman in the video had grown into an international superstar.

"When there was an argument and her father picked up something, she would come and stand in front of me and do like this," her mother said, spreading her arms like wings. "She was so young and just trying to protect me."

Maybe because of the realities of her life at home, Nicki continued to use her imagination as a means to escape.

"To get away from all their fighting, I would imagine being a new person. Cookie was my first identity...that stayed with me for a while. I went on to Harajuku Barbie, then Nicki Minaj. Fantasy Nicki Minaj...Growing Up was my reality. I must have been such a fucking annoying little girl...

Everywhere we went I was up singing or acting, like, 'Hey look at me!''

At the age of 12, Nicki heard her older neighbor rapping. This prompted Nicki to try writing something of her own.

"I was like, how did you learn how to do that? I went home and wrote Cookie's the Name and Chocolate Chip is the Flavor, the infamous rap, and I waited until she got home, knocked on her door and I spit the rap to her...She called the neighborhood guys and she was like, 'yo, come and listen to her rap. I was thinking she liked the rap, but she was trying to play me, trying to say the rap was so wack. But I was so young. I didn't know. They kept making me say it over and over. They definitely gave me the energy to continue spitting that rap, but they were clearly laughing behind my back.''

Years later, the writer of "Cookie's The Name and Chocolate Chip is The Flavor" would be laughing as well.....

Laughing all the way to the bank, that is.

When she got to high school, she auditioned at Fiorello H. LaGuardia High School, also known as Fame High School. She had originally wanted to sing, but had lost her voice prior to auditioning. Before giving up, her mother did something that may have altered the course of music history and Hip Hop culture forever.

Nicki Miraj would go on to tell E!

"I auditioned for singing, but I didn't get in because I hurt my voice, I was like, Oh, my God. Get me out of here."

Carol would go on to tell E!

"She was so sad…She said, 'Mommy, I want to go home.' I said, 'No, no, there is one more thing. There is the drama. You have to try out for that."

Nicki would say:

"I was used to getting my way, but that was the one thing I remember my mother putting her foot down, I stomped my feet all the way down to the basement where the drama department resides. Within the first 20 minutes I knew that was where I wanted to be. I didn't feel uncomfortable. I didn't feel weird and I got in as a drama major. Thank God she made me stay."

While at Fiorello H. LaGuardia High School, Nicki was established herself as being outgoing in an entire school of outgoing kids, putting years of role playing to use to stand out amongst her peers, further developing the skills that she would putting to use in her future career.

"To be in a room with a hundred kids and all

doing a British accent and they've never been to the U.K., I was like how do you know how to do that? I thought I was the only one."

Years later, she would tell E! that not only did most of the White students think that she was crazy, but that there were only three Black students in her entire class.

"All the white people thought I was crazy, I called Ashley Bashley. Andrew I would call him Bandrew. That made me feel better. It quenched some mental thirst and they loved it."

After high school, Nicki made an attempt at becoming a professional actress, but it didn't work out the way she had hoped. While waitressing at a Red Lobster restaurant in 2001, Nicki played one of her last gigs in "In Case You Forget", an off off Broadway play.

"It just didn't pan out, I lost the passion for it. I wanted everything really quickly. I went on two auditions. I was like, 'what? I didn't get that role? Oh, forget this.' I'm done. They don't realize who I am?"

Like so many others, Nicki was soon met face to face with the realities of a normal work life. From waitressing, to working various office jobs, such as being an office manager for a Wall Street firm, she knew that she was destined for something greater. After getting fired from a job, Nicki made the risky decision to become a music artist.

"I had never given anything my all, I was like, 'you know what, 'I don't care if I end up in a shelter, I'm not going back to work.'"

Valerie Mitchell

CHAPTER TWO
Nicki's Delight

Nicki became a part of a Hip Hop group known as "The Hoodstar$", which included Hip Hop artists Scaff Beezy (Safaree "SB" Samuels), Lou$tar, and 7even Up, signing a deal with the group "Full Force". The Hoodstar$ would go on to record the entrance song for Diva Victoria, of WWE fame. The name of the song was "Don't Mess With", and it was featured on the compilation album with other songs and artists, called ThemeAddict: WWE The Music, Vol. 6. Nicki would soon leave the group, releasing her own material onto her own personal Myspace page.

Fendi, Dirty Money Entertainment's CEO, came across Nicki's Myspace page.

According Nicki Minaj's Bing Music biography:

"It was there that Dirty Money Entertainment CEO Fendi first heard her ability to freestyle and first laid eyes on her steamy set of promo shots"

* * *

According to E!, Fendi is the one who advised Nicki to go by Nicki Minaj, instead of Nicki Maraj.

"My real name is Maraj. Fendi flipped it when he met me because I had such a nasty flow! I eat bitches!" -Nicki Minaj

Through her connection with Fendi, Nicki appeared on his "The Come Up" DVD series, which happened to feature both Nicki and Lil Wayne in Volume 11.

On the subject of how he wound up discovering Nicki Minaj, Lil Wayne would go on to tell E! :

"I was like this female right here is amazing... She'd be amazing for my label as well. That's when I knew I wanted to sign her... I was like get me in contact with that girl named Nicki."

Nicki Minaj would say:

"He was smitten with me, I guess you could say that. His people reached out to my people. They happened to know each other. The next thing you know I was flying out to meet him and he was

telling me about something called Young Money. I was like, who?"

CHAPTER THREE

Rise of The Barbie

Beginning in 2007 and ending in 2009, Nicki had a mixtape run, releasing "Playtime Is Over" via Dirty Money Records, "Suka Free" with Be, and the infamous "Beam Me Up Scotty" via Trapaholics Records. In 2008, she won "Female Artist of The Year" at the 2008 Underground Music Awards.

She featured on Lil Wayne's Dedication 3, as well as on remixes of other artists' records. In 2009, it was announced that Nicki Minaj had signed a record deal with Young Money/Universal, retaining ownership of money earned from sponsorships, endorsements, merchandise, tours, and her publishing (things that are increasingly rare for a modern mainstream artist to keep).

In a press release announcing Nicki Minaj's signing to Young Money Entertainment / Universal, Lil Wayne would say:

* * *

"I am honored to have Nicki Minaj as Young Money's First Lady...She is a star."

In the press release, a newly signed, Young Money Entertainment artist Nicki Minaj would say:

"To say I'm excited would be an understatement...It's validation. It's proof. It's empowerment. I represent every little girl in a hood near you. To everyone that supported me two years ago when I was on underground mix-tapes and DVDs and to the people that only caught on two weeks ago, I say thank you. Be proud of yourself. You've given girls all around the world the permission to change the face of female rap."

Nicki's mother, Carol Maraj, would go on to say this on the subject of Nicki Minaj's signing to Lil Wayne's Young Money Entertainment:

"Nicki's success changed my life drastically ... Her success gave me a new outlook on life. We were living in Jamaica, Queens, and Nicki was talking to me and telling me Lil' Wayne was interested in her music and paying her a lot of attention. I told her we just have to pray on it. That God wouldn't bring her this far and not see it through. I told her God was going to complete it. I prayed and then I told her it is done! When she called me with the news she was so excited.

We were all blown away by her success."

"It took a lot to help me prepare my mind…But I realized that it was time to start following my dream. When Nicki got her break I didn't have to work so hard anymore. I was able to relax and take care of me. All those years, I was going through so much and still running to work, every day, from nine-to-five. Because of Nicki I was now able to focus on me."

CHAPTER FOUR
Pink Friday

Nicki Minaj's first official album under Young Money Entertainment / Universal, "Pink Friday", was released to the public on November 19, 2010. "Your Love", her first single, not only hit number 14 on Billboard's Hot 100s, but also cracked the Top 10 Hot R&B/Hip-Hop songs, and if that weren't impressive enough, she was also not only the first female rapper to be on the charts unaccompanied since Missy Elliot in 2002, but was also the first female rapper to be included amongst MTV's "Hottest MCs".

According to MTV :

"In the summer of 2010, Nicki was the acid-tongued "two" to Drake's "one" in Lil Wayne's Young Money one-two punch...With her debut album still on the way, she was murdering features left and right...

* * *

MTV News' Director of Hip Hop News, Rahman Dukes, said this about Nicki Minaj:

"When she hit the scene, she was just like the pretty girl alongside Wayne...Drake was really the next one that everyone was looking out for."

The album featured Hip Hop artist Eminem as his controversial alter ego "Slim Shady", responsible for offending quite a few people in the first half of the 2000's, and of course more all throughout his highly successful career, on the standout song "Roman's Revenge". Surprisingly, it wasn't Slim Shady who drew the most ire this time around, but Nicki's own British accent using alter ego, "Roman Zolanski".

"Word that bitch mad 'cause I took the spot/ Well, bitch, if you ain't sh——-ing, then get off the pot/ Got some n——-az out in Brooklyn that'll off your top.' "

The general consensus was that she was dissing Lil Kim, who reigned throughout the 90's and early 2000's as Hip Hop royalty. While on The Wendy Williams Show, Nicki was asked about the song.

"I don't get into that, ... I feel like my music, my fans know everything that's going on. Every time I talk, every time I spit raps, my fans know who I'm talking about, what I'm talking about. I don't have to sit up here and detail it. No. For what?"

* * *

Nicki Minaj also said the song is directed towards:

"everyone who has been in interviews talking.....no one is worth having their name mentioned out of my mouth and they never will get that."

Lil Kim would go on to release a mixtape called "Black Friday", a play off of Nicki Minaj's "Pink Friday". Foxy Brown would even join the fray, releasing "Hold Yuh" and "Massacre", before her and Nicki squashed their beef in June 2012, and Minaj would tell MTV News:

"I never really told Foxy how much she has influenced me and how much she changed my life, and you've gotta tell people that when they're alive to even be able to take the compliment, instead of paying tribute to them when they're no longer here"

Nicki Minaj also said that Foxy Brown is:
"the most influential female rapper"

She would also tell Rap-Up:

"I really loved [Foxy] as a female rapper. I was really interested in her mind and her aura [and] I was really, really into Jay-Z. Me and my friends

in high school, we were reciting all of the Jay lyrics. His words were our words in our conversations all the time."

She has described Roman as her demonic, gay twin brother that lives inside of her. After winning Best Hip Hop video at the MTV VMAs, she had this to say about Roman's "involvement" on her next album, "Prink Friday: Roman Reloaded".

According to The Hollywood Reporter, Nicki Minaj said this, on the subject of Roman being on her next album:

"The new album is going to have a lot of Roman on it...And if you're not familiar with Roman, then you will be familiar with him very soon . He's the boy that lives inside of me. He's a lunatic and he's gay and he'll be on there a lot."

"Everybody knows my favorite alter ego is Roman, He's bad. That's why I like Roman. I think I started liking Roman more because everybody else starting like Roman, so he became my favorite. People are expecting him to do some real craziness on the next album."

***

In a March 2012 interview with Complex Magazine's Miss Info, Nicki Minaj described how different she was to people in the industry, and how she doesn't rehearse what she does in her music videos.

"No, I hate rehearsing...I never rehearse what I'm

gonna do in a video. It's just that I have this love-hate

relationship with the camera. I wanna please the camera so bad. The perfectionist in my brain is like, "You have to be on." I always want to feel like I gave everything my all and never,

never, never exhibit laziness."

She describes herself as not being the typical music artist that so many others in the industry assumed that she would be.

"In the beginning people thought they knew who I was but they didn't...They tried to create something. Whenever I'm being me, the people love it. They connect with it. But whenever I find myself in a situation ... prime example, during a photo shoot, if a photographer is telling me every little thing to do, I shut down. And you might as well kiss the photo shoot goodbye. I'm an artist in every motherfucking sense of the word. I work well with people who trust my instinct and

understand that I am the marketer and promoter of the Nicki

Minaj brand. This did not come overnight. This did not happen
from a record company. No manager created this."

Nicki has been quoted as saying this, in regards to her style:

"What people don't know is that before I was doing that craziness I was doing me, I was just doing regular sounding rap that anyone could hear and identify with. But once I started doing all that weird shit—I'm not mad at it because it got everyone's attention."

The single "I'm The Best" was released, to critical acclaim. When the single "Massive Attack" was released as a test run however, it was a comparative dud.

According to a 2010 Vibe article:

"Massive Attack, the Sean Garrett-produced track that left a lot of people scratching their heads, it seems as though she is still figuring that out. It's the kind of song that makes you feel old — like you're missing something that the kids on designer drugs might understand...Or maybe it's just not a very good song. Either way, the response has been lukewarm at best."

***

Sean Garrett would then defend the song, saying

"Massive Attack was the record she wanted to go with. I think it's a different sound. She wanted to make a statement. She definitely has a different direction for her album and her career than where most people think she wants to go."

Speaking with Vibe, Nicki would offer her own take on the song.

"It was important for me to do something not everyone thought I was gonna do ... People close to me have their preferences, their favorite Nicki thing, and I have to stand up sometimes and block out the noise."

In January of 2011, Nicki appeared as a musical guest on Saturday Night Live and performed "Moment 4 Life" and "Right Thru Me". Because of this, her popularity grew even further, catapulting her album to the coveted number 1 spot on the Billboard 200 list only a month later. She released the single, which was really just a bonus track on the album, "Super Bass" in May of that same year, and it went to number 8, later becoming four times platinum. The song's popularity was assisted by both Taylor Swift and Selena Gomez, two hugely popular mega stars, who rapped the lyrics to the song. Nicki would even open up for Britney Spears on the Femme Fatale Tour.

***

A month within it's release, Pink Friday was certified platinum by the RIAA in the U.S.

Marc Hogan, in a review of the album for Spin, said this about Nicki Minaj and her new album:

"Nicki Minaj will not be contained...Not to 16-bar verses. Not to one persona. Not even to hip-hop. Brought up in Jamaica, Queens, and taught to be a star at New York City's "Fame" school (LaGuardia High School of Music & Art and Performing Arts), the MC born Onika Maraj has more alter egos than most pop stars have nicknames. With three promising mixtapes and a streak of spotlight-hogging guest verses, she's established herself as the best (avowedly bisexual) female in hip-hop's "no homo" boys' club. But anyone who comes to her official full-length, Pink Friday, expecting more of the raw, terrifically unhinged rhyming that stole Kanye West's "Monster" will be disappointed. Rap's most hotly anticipated debut works best if you don't think of it as a rap album at all...albeit with less Auto-Tune and a lot less innuendo, Minaj turns toward frothy, hooky pop on her new album. That means you'll hear her singing, which is nothing exceptional, as well as rapping, which is still spectacular: cartoonish, clever, and endlessly flexible."

CHAPTER FIVE
Barbie

After her songs on her second album, "Pink Friday: Roman Reloaded" were leaked, Nicki, having over 13 million followers on Twitter, and being active within her community of fans on the social site, did what was unthinkable to most, especially in an age of the music industry that relies so heavily on the social media and networking aspects of The Internet. Nicki Minaj, Hip Hop mega star deleted her Twitter account.

"Like seriously, it's but so much a person can take. Good f* cking bye,"

-Nicki, shortly before deleting her twitter account.

Regarding the situation, OMG would go on to report this:

"It looked like the pop star was only going to reprimand the site in question— called

NickiDaily.com, which now appears to be shut down— for illegally distributing the songs from Nicki's Pink Friday: Roman Reloaded album, when she blocked it from her Twitter account... But eventually she decided to leave all of her followers out in the cold. Talk about one bad apple spoiling the bunch!"

In regards to this situation, E would go on to report that Nicki Minaj said this:

"A voice in my head told me to delete my Twitter and that's what I did...I had 13 million followers and I hope they will wait for me. I reply all the time and get to know them by name and I have a really personal bond with them... not all 13 million, but at least 10 of them a day."

Many of her fans clamored to have her back on twitter.

OMG reported that some of her numerous fans tweeted:

"Nope. Nope Stop playing @NICKIMINAJ WE NEED YOU,"

"We learned our lesson. we took lots of things for granted. NOT NO MORE. PLEASE COME BACK!"

"That depressing moment when you go to @NICKIMINAJ account and it says this user does

not exist :(

Eventually, Nicki Minaj returned to Twitter, with her account being restored the way it was before.

In a 2010 Pitchfork review, Tom Breihan wrote this, in regards to Nicki Minaj's work on "Monster".

"Nicki's been a magnetic, polarizing, scene-stealing figure for something like a year, but her masterfully manic verse here feels like the moment where she becomes a full-on star, an undeniable force in rap...She's a whirlwind of energy , showing her full repertoire of nutso voices and kicking the living fuck out of the beat, sounding like she's having an absolute blast the whole time: 'Yeah, I'm in that Tonka, color of Willy Wonka! You could be the king but watch the queen conquer!'

In August, 2011, Nicki Minaj had added one more notch on the figurative belt worn by so many other celebrity actresses and musicians. She had a nipple slip / wardrobe malfunction. Nicki would apologize for the nipple slip / wardrobe malfunction on ABC's Nightline show.

The Associated Press reported this, regarding the matter:

"ABC News is apologizing for a wardrobe malfunction that gave singer Nicki Minaj more

exposure than she bargained for. Nicki appeared Friday on the "Good Morning America" concert series, wearing a loose-fitting halter top that she occasionally had to adjust. As Nicki sang "Where Dem Girls At," some slips made one of her nipples fleetingly visible. Despite a five-second delay, the slips were seen during the East Coast's live telecast. ABC said they were edited out of Friday's later feeds to other parts of the country."

Tim Winter, President of the Parents Television Council said,

"the Parents Television Council has something to say about Nicki Minaj's wardrobe malfunction this morning. For the umpteenth time in recent memory a morning news show has included inappropriate content for children and families."

For years, rumors were going around that Nicki Minaj is gay. She had this to say about the subject of whether or not she was bisexual:

"That's definitely not true....I guess some people are thrown off by me embracing gay culture. But I don't feel the need to explain that. Unless someone asks me a specific question."

In 2012, Nicki was featured on pop cultural icon Madonna's album, on the single "Give Me All Your Love". Madonna gave Nicki a small kiss on the lips on Nicki's 29th birthday party, shortly after wrapping up the music video for "Give Me All Your Love". Afterward, Nicki would tweet:

"OH MY Finggg Gahhhhh!!!!! MADONNA jus kissed me!!!!! On the lips!!!!!!! It felt Sooooo good. Soooo soft!!!! *passes out* aaahhhhh!!!!!!!!!"

On Nicki's multitude of personalities, such as Roman Polanski, Harajuku Barbie, Nicki the Ninja, Martha Polanski, etc., David Wallace-Wells, in New York Magazine, wrote:

"And all of whom are dressed to the nines, in an à la carte assemblage of Cyndi Lauper gone cyberpunk, sexed-up Missy Elliott, black-light anime, Japanese street fashion, and hip-hop booty mag. Among a laundry pile of other influences from the anything-goes fashion future... The whole circus is dazzling and code-cracking genius, since pop markets run by the same laws as any other: grow or die. The problem of being sexy in rap has forced all of Nicki's flummoxed emcee predecessors the other way, into little whirlpools of self-caricature. (See, along with Kim and Elliott, MC Lyte, Da Brat, and Foxy Brown.) She shuns comparisons to her contemporary Lady Gaga, although both have transformed a generation with their corybantic performances and colorful outfits."

Speaking to ABC's Juju Chang, in April of 2012, on Nightline, Nicki Minaj would respond with this, in regards to the comparisons to acclaimed pop star sensation, Lady Gaga.

"We're in completely different lanes...I'm a rapper ... Gaga's a fantastic artist, you know, she paved her way. She's opened her own lane. But I think that I have my own lane. And we never cross. Ever. So, you know, I really don't get the comparison anymore. Our music doesn't sound the same. Our stage presence is not the same. I just can't see the similarities"

Some would beg to differ, as one major thing that both Nicki and Lady Gaga had in common during this time period, was their outlandish style and fashion sense. They both definitely knew how to draw attention with their off the wall outfits (or at least, their stylists did). One such example was in September of 2011, when Nicki attended the iHeartRadio Music Festival wearing a chicken wing necklace. MTV described Nicki and her necklace as

"...paired with an embellished pink tutu dress, hot pink bra, space-age tights, larger -than-life blonde permed hair, and plastic neon accessories."

"The most uh-mazing thing about this particular necklace is that it has totally been Minaj-ified," according to Chrissy Mahlmeister,

for MTV. "It's HOT PINK. Like, what screams Barbie more than that? Nothing. Also, paired with a buttload of gold chains makes it absolutely POIFECT for Ms. Minaj. Just when we thought it couldn't get any better than her sporting ice cream and a soft pretzel around her neck, Nicki pulled out ALL the stops with this edible accessory."

According to Billboard, Mattel (yes, that Mattel) created a one of a kind Nicki Minaj Barbie, and auctioned it off on Charitybuzz.com, starting the bid at $1,000.

Billboard would go on to say:

"The Barbie itself is a pink explosion, with mini-Minaj decked out in towering boots, signature long hair and an outfit made of sparkly toule and diamonds.

According to Billboard, a spokesman for Barbie, by the name of Stefani Yocky, said this:

"Barbie is obviously a pop culture icon. She's been in the spotlight for over 50 years, and strikes that chord with girls of all ages in terms of being representative of the times. And Nicki is a big part of pop culture and also huge within the fashion industry, as well as a big Barbie fan."

CHAPTER SIX

The Smell of The Rain

Nicki Minaj was the first female Hip Hop rapper to have a position on the Forbes' Cash Kings List, because she made an estimated $6.5 million dollars in 2011.

Of Nicki Minaj's placement on Forbes' Cash Kings List, Vibe wrote:

"Making her debut at #13 on Cash Kings 2011, Nicki Minaj is snatching up more than personal achievements…"

"She's the first female rapper to ever grace the list earning $6.5 million in the past 365 sitting above B.o.B. and Pitbull"

In fact, Nicki would go on to make the Forbes Cash Kings List four times in a row, placing 8th on the list, in 2012 (with **$15.5 million** made), fourth place in 2013

($29 million made) and made the list again in 2014 **($14 million made).**

Can someone say..... **BALLING!?**

Not bad at all, for a woman who **grew up** as a young girl in South Jamaica, Queens.

On February 12, 2012, Nicki Minaj was at the famous Staples Center in the city of Los Angeles, in the state of California. Why, you ask? Because that's where the 54th Grammy Awards Ceremony was being held at, and Nicki was scheduled to perform there. She walked the red carpet wearing a red robe, and was being escorted by an older man who was dressed up as a pope. She would perform the songs "Roman's Revenge " and "Roman Holiday". Her performance had an exorcism and dancing priests. Furthering the comparisons between Nicki Minaj and Lady Gaga, Laurieann Gibson, Lady Gaga's former choreographer, helped put the ensemble together, and had this to say about the situation, telling MTV News:

"Nicki Minaj was so much fun for me, and it was like a real breath of fresh air , and musically, to get back to the rap game, to see a female MC dominate the pop charts, this, historically, for me, I feel a bit of responsibility...When I did 'The Rain,' that video for Missy [Elliott], and just with Puff and the evolution of Bad Boy Records and my responsibility there and the pressure to maintain dominant rappers [on major award shows] and not let them lose street credibility,

the years of all that torture ... and all of those moments. When I got back to Nicki, I was so happy to be in that soulful music again, in that fight, in the idea that rap is not dead and that somebody like her can be many things in many genres and not be limited...I love [when] I heard Roman Reloaded. I loved her delivery. I love the way she flows...So the Pink Friday Tour is really good and it's kind of like a glimpse back to what a real rap show is. It's intimate but big at the same time."

According to CBS New York. Bill Donohue, President of the Catholic League, reportedly said

"Perhaps the most vulgar was the sexual statement that showed a scantily clad female dancer stretching backwards while an altar boy knelt between her legs in prayer,"

Nicki would tell the Associated Press:

"I don't know what is the big issue? You know how people write plays and movies? That's what I did. I wrote that and I gave the world a tiny little preview of what was to come. And so I have to perform it on the set in which it would be in the movie, right?"

Her controversial, yet genius, antics made her even more of a celebrity than ever before, further propelling her towards even more mainstream success, much as similar tactics had been done previously by Lady Gaga and Madonna. CBS' "This Morning" was told by Ken Ehrlich, who executive produces the Grammys:

"Look, one of the things that is always very important to us, we don't like to restrict an artist's creative freedom...She came to us with that idea. Often the ideas are ours, sometimes they're the acts we work with."

"At that one? I didn't say great...I looked at that one and said, OK, I knew about her alter ego, I'm kind of aware of what that was, and I definitely had some questions about it."

CHAPTER SEVEN

Reloading

On April 3, 2012, Nicki Minaj's "Pink Friday: Roman Reloaded", was released in the United States and, according to Nielsen Soundscan (the most frequently cited source of music sales), sold 253,000, which was better than what industry analysts had predicted it to sell. Their predictions placed Nicki's "Pink Friday: Roman Reloaded" album to sell between 215,000 and 235,000 copies. Although it was her second official album, the album hit number 1 on the Billboard 200, also marking her second album in a row that reached number 1 on the Billboard 200. She hit number one in Japand, and "Pink Friday: Roman Reloaded" also propelled her into becoming the first female rap artist to debut at number one on the U.K. Charts. Nicki had also become the first female solo music artist to have at least seven singles on the Billboard top 100 at the exact same time.

Nicki's second album, "Pink Friday: Roman Reloaded"'s powerhouse jump towards number one slot on the charts may have caused a casualty. Nicki's friend, Madonna's album, MDNA. Madonna's MDNA was previously on the number slot, when it was knocked from off of it's perch by Nicki Minaj's own sophomore album, "Pink Friday: Roman Reloaded". Madonna's DNA album sells fell 86.7 percent, from number one, down to number eight. Billboard reported that since Nielsen SoundScan started tracking sales way back in 1991, this was the largest drop in the largest second week percentage wise for a number 1 debuting album. Lady Gaga's "Born This Way" had held the previous record, falling 84.27 percent it's second week. The week that it was released, Lady Gaga's "Born This Way" had sold a whoppingly impressive 1.11 million copies, which is an increasingly rare thing to do in the era of downloadable music and file sharing, only to sell "only" 174,000 copies during it's second week.

Nicki Minaj tells Miss Info, in a March 2012 interview with Complex Magazine:

"Doing the Super Bowl with Madonna doesn't really change Nicki Minaj's personal goals...My goal right now is still to put out "Pink Friday: Roman Reloaded", sell five million copies eventually, and tour every country in the world. That's what I've been working toward. So while the world is talking about, 'Oh my God, I can't believe Nicki Minaj was at the Super Bowl!' I'm mixing and mastering my music. In my scheme of things it's way bigger.' "

* * *

Nicki would go on to surprise her twitter fans with this tweeted message:

"I am ABSOLUTELY in LOVE w/ this f@%# ing ALBUM!!!!!!! Like!!! AbsoFCNGlutely in LOVE barbz!!!!!!!!!!!!!"

Nicki Minaj's "Pink Friday: Roman Reloaded" album was a Young Money Entertainment / Universal Republic Records release. Production credits included Rico Beats, Kenoe, RedOne, Hit Boy, Ester Dean, Oak and Flip.

For features on Nicki Minaj's "Pink Friday: Roman Reloaded" she wound up recruiting a plethora of talented, unique, and artistic individuals, including 2 Chainz, Nas, Young Jeezy, Bobby V, Chris Brown, Rick Ross, Cam'ron, and Beenie Man, as well as fellow Young Money Entertainment label mates Drake and her mentor, the multiplatinum Lil Wayne aka Lil Weezy.

The album was split into two different parts, with the first half being more Hip Hop oriented, and the second half consisting of more Pop oriented music.

Producer Andrew "Pop" Wansel, son of legendary musician, Dexter Wansel, and who also worked with Nicki Minaj on "Your Love", would tell Rap Up this:

"There's more surprises this time…I think she's proven, like, 'Yo, I can rap. I'm probably the best girl to really do this shit ever .' Now she's

more comfortable and she's having a little more fun."

Cash Money Records A&R Joshua Berkman talked about the creation of Nicki Minaj's "Pink Friday: Roman Reloaded" album with HitQuarters.

"With Nicki specifically, it's all about the particular sound she wants and not everybody can make that sound...She's very particular about her beats and wouldn't just rap or sing on anything— I could give her a thousand tracks and she may only like one or two."

"With Nicki you have to give all the credit to Wayne...Wayne was the one that was in with all the Young Money artists every single night, teaching them. That's how the whole Young Money album [' We Are Young Money'] came about. He's the genius behind that. But most of all you have to give it to her for being such an incredible artist and hard worker."

Clover Hope, Senior Editor at Vibe, asked Nicki to simplify the description for the album.

"It's going in a very free , exhilarating direction in terms of me owning who I am and me enjoying the process of making music...I think that when you get the album you'll feel as if I had absolutely no boundaries. That's probably the best way to explain it so that you understand.

The album just has no boundaries. The album cannot be boxed in."

Clover Hope seemed to want Nicki to give more info.

"You know what, I cannot break my album down into how the normal person like yourself would break an album down and say, well this is rap and this is pop. There is no rap or pop for me. It's Nicki Minaj. It's one collective body of amazing work. You'll feel it. I don't like the labels because sometimes just by one word or one label, a person can take that the wrong way and apply a negative spin to that. So I don't give my music labels."

Rolling Stone's Jody Rosen had this to say about Nicki Minaj:

"Nicki Minaj is a purist's nightmare. She doesn't just straddle pop categories; she dumps them in a Cuisinart, whips them to a frothy purée, and then trains a guided missile at the whole mess. She is a rapper's rapper, a master of flow and punch lines, with skills to please the most exacting gatekeepers of hip-hop street cred. But she's a bubblegum starlet as well, delivering confections to the nation's mall rats. "I'm in the HOV lane," Nicki boasts on her second LP. It's true: She's one of the few performers who can rival Jay-Z's blend of artistic bona fides and

sheer star power. But Nicki is also in the Gaga lane, the Bowie lane, the Missy Elliott and Gary Glitter and Katy Perry and Betty Boop lanes. (By the sound of "Right by My Side"— a blustery duet with Chris Brown— she can cruise in the Jordin Sparks lane, too.) Then there's the Roman Zolanski lane . "Roman Reloaded" opens with Minaj —a biracial woman from Queens via Trinidad— ranting in the voice of her (Polish?) homosexual "twin brother" alter ego. In the same song, she takes on the voice of Martha Zolanski, Roman's mother, singing in a cartoon Cockney accent. "Take your medication, Roman," counsels Minaj/Martha. "Quack, quack to a duck and a chicken, too/Put the hyena in a freakin' zoo," answers Minaj/ Roman. Later, she bursts into "O Come, All Ye Faithful."

She's just limbering up. On *Roman Reloaded*, the energy never flags – it's the rare filler-free mega-pop album, an achievement for a record that stretches to 19 songs and 69 minutes. Minaj fans dismayed by her post-"Super Bass" turn toward pop will be cheered up by the red-meat hip-hop here. There's booming triumphalism ("Champion"), electro-rap boastfests ("Beez in the Trap") and a couple of collaborations with her mentor Lil Wayne, in which she more than justifies the claim that ends the album: "I am the female Weezy."

48

Rich Juzwiak, in a review for Gawker, said this about
the album:

**"It contained little sense of what Nicki Minaj
was other than a pop star who sometimes rapped
and sometimes did so cleverly"**

**"Roman Reloaded is the Wicked Witch of the
West to its predecessor's East. It's worse than the
other one was.**

**The stakes feel higher here because Pink
Friday helped turn Nicki Minaj into a standalone
superstar. Now is the time to assert herself and
yet this album finds Nicki more fractured than
ever. From the start, she's flaunted her duality,
turning decades of the multitasking burden put
on women in hip-hop into a marketing tool that
allows her to be potentially all things to all
people. (It's a grand tradition she's capitalizing
on."**

The "Pink Friday: Roman Reloaded Tour" launched in
May 2012 and was to have over 40 shows in Asia, Europe,
North American, and Australia.

CHAPTER EIGHT

Reloaded

On May 25, Nicki Minaj performed in Tokyo, Japan for her "Pink Friday: Roman Reloaded", and unfortunately, one of her fans was murdered after attending the show. On May 25, 21 year old Nicola Furlong, a foreign exchange student from Ireland's Dublin City University, was found dead in a hotel in Tokyo, after she had attended Nicki Minaj's concert at Zepp Tokyo, several hours earlier. PerezHilton.com reported that Nicola Furlong and Sarah Maher, who is Nicola Furlong's friend, had met up with one of Nicki Minaj's backup dancers, James Blackston and a music artist by the name of Larry Perry after the show, and went to the artists' hotel rooms.

Sara Maher would later say that she was sexually assaulted by both Nicki Minaj's backup dancer, James Blackston, and the musician Larry Perry, in a taxi.

Nicola Furlong was found strangled to dead inside of the hotel room.

* * *

Shortly afterward, on May 31, Nicki Minaj sent her condolences via Twitter, also denying allegations that one of her dancers was involved in the murder of her fan.

"Saddened to learn one of my precious fans; found tragically murdered in Japan. My love & prayers are with the family of Nicola Furlong"

Nicki then tweeted directly to Perez Hilton, denying the involvement of anyone in her entourage, and crew.

"My dancers had nothing to do w/ this tragedy. No one in my entourage was questioned or arrested. They all flew home from Japan,"

"That person on your [site] is NOT my dancer. We do NOT know the men in custody. Too much misleading information."

Nearly a week later, Nicki Minaj's "Pink Friday: Roman Reloaded" garnered even more criticism, because of it's pop oriented elements. Peter Rosenberg, one of famed Hip Hop radio station Hot 97's DJs, blasted Nicki Minaj's song, "Starships", for it's pop appeal at that year's Summer Jam.

"Now hold on, before I get to the real hip-hop shit of the day, because I see the real hip-hop

heads sprinkled in here, I see 'em. I know there's some chicks here waiting to sing 'Starships' later, I'm not talking to y'all right now, fuck that bullshit. I'm here to talk about real hip-hop shit. People here to see A$AP Rocky today. People here to see ScHoolboy Q on this stage. That's that shit I represent."

Lil Wayne would then pull Nicki from the Summer Jam lineup, and she then responded to Rosenberg on twitter. A year later, they reconciled on Hot 97, with Rosenberg telling Nicki:

"I am sorry that things went as left as they did and I never had ill feelings about you as a human being, ever...I would have never ever dissed you in any personal way beyond my distaste for that song."

Nicki responded with:

"It's cool...It's water under the bridge. It was so long ago, I can't even act like I care anymore."

"In hindsight I should have done [Summer Jam] because it was my hometown...I wish I would've just come out. I apologize for not doing the show."

"I don't know your resume. I never found you funny. I never found you entertaining. I never found you smart...I just found you annoying. To me it was like, who are you? You don't have enough of a resume to make those comments."

Years later, in a 2014 interview with Radiolab,

52

Rosenberg would explain:

"I thought she was really good, in fact I though she was the total package...The year before it all happened, I pulled her aside at Summer Jam (2011) and I said, 'Hey, I think you could be the greatest female artist of all time, the greatest female rapper of all time. And I just want you to know in thinking that, I'm going hold you to a high standard so I probably will say things about you.'"

"Starships is a blatant pop song so I didn't like the song," he said. "In the moment it felt like, you're a Hip Hop star, why would you do this? This is not for us. When core Hip Hop artists make pop songs it upsets me because it can be a moment that blurs and messes up Hip Hop."

The London Daily Mail's Ross McDonagh reported that Nicki Minaj had went to a Portuguese themed restaurant called Nando's, ordering $4,700 worth of chicken.

According the the London Daily Mail, Nicki Minaj, while on tour, has been known to order breakfast food items such as Belgian waffles, large fruit platters, strawberries, turkey bacon, scrambled egg whites, and assorted juices. The London Daily Mail has attributed the ordering of spicy fried chicken, lots of chicken wings, but zero thighs, deli trays filled with cold meats, and large cheese platters, to Nicki Minaj.

* * *

"[My dressing room] looks like something out of Aladdin,"

"Pink flowers and candles, white rugs, couches covered in pink satin."

"I eat olives with a towel on! No word on Nado's chicken!

"I have a big, colorful gun that I spray the audience with, I don't tell anyone what I'm spraying. It's a mystery!"

"In the first act, I have three layers of clothes on. Then I just strip down as I go. I have about 100 wigs,'

-Nicki Minaj, to People magazine, on the subject of her "Pink Friday: Roman Reloaded" tour.

PerezHilton.com would report that Nicki Minaj was allegedly conned out of $100,000 by a Trinidadian Producer during the filming of her music video for the song called "Pound The Alarm", in Nicki Minaj's homeland of Trinidad. He was hired to help things out on the production side of things, and he allegedly did not do the services that he was hired for. The producer, on the other hand, claim that what Nicki Minaj said was false, and that he is actually owed $19,000.

In July 2012, during Nicki Minaj's "Pink Friday:

Roman Reloaded Tour", for the third consecutive year, Nicki Minaj was awarded BET's coveted "Best Female Hip-Hop Artist" award.

"I really, really appreciate BET for keeping this category alive, and I appreciate all the female rappers doing their thing, past, present, and future…"
-Nicki Minaj, on her winning Best Female Hip Hop Artist.

Teen magazine interviewed Nicki, asking her about her voice acting role that she had in 20the Century Fox's movie "Ice Age: Continental Drift", where she played Seffie, the wooly mammoth.

"It was fun! It was funny and heartwarming… It was very, very intense in 3D. The teeth, jaws, and paws of the animals felt like they were right there in your face. But it was fun. I had a great experience….I was more excited than surprised…I didn't care what they wanted me to play; I was definitely going to play it. I'm really, really honored to be a part of the movie. Even with just a small role, I'm honored and excited to be a part of something that's been around for such a long time. I mean, this is the fourth installment, so it was a big deal for me. I think my character is pretty cool. She has a little flower in her hair. She is a mammoth, but she's a beautiful mammoth…In the movie, he's kind of the popular guy and I'm kind of the popular girl,

and I secretly have a little crush on him...I'm kind of like the loud mouth that tries to prevent him from liking another mammoth in the movie."

"Ice Age: Continental Drift" would debut, in July 2012, at the number one spot at the box office, collecting $46 million dollars.

Nicki Minaj would go on to tweet this about the release of the movie:

"#IceAge4 Continental Drift is everywhere today!!!! :)"

Nicki Minaj's Young Money Entertainment label mate and friend, Drake, would also tweet about the film, saying this on twitter about it's release:

"ICE AGE 4 today!! Can't wait to see it. I feel like I gave my mammoth a silky Leon Phelps voice. Enjoy kids"

In March of 2012, Nicki Minaj told Complex Magazine that she has plans to be married and have children by 2022, and that she wants to have a boy, instead of having a girl.

"In 2022, I'll definitely be married and I'll definitely have my two children....Yeah, 'cause you think I'm going to dress her up in wigs, no. [Laughs] I really need a boy in my life. A baby

boy. Because...I'm so attached to my little brother and I felt like that was my real son. And boys, they're just so, I don't know...My heart just melts when I see them."

Nicki Minaj was quoted as saying this, on the subject of if she will still be working in the year 2022:

"I always said There's no way I could still be doing rap, 'cause what will I still be talking about? But now that the public has given me this opportunity to do all types of music, I might have more longevity. As long as I can continue to experiment, then I might be doing music in 10 years. I know that I don't feel like I *need* to be doing music in 10 years to feel fulfilled. And I don't want to be one of those people who doesn't know when to call it quits. Let's just say that."

"It's just about you and your heart. When you're still relevant to the culture. But who am I to know? I'm only on my second album. Maybe you never get that memo in your brain that tells you, Quit it. I would enjoy a career like Jay-Z's, where he raps because he wants to, not 'cause he has to. I think that's the scary part when, after 10 years in the game, people can't pay their bills and now you're desperate. And so that's why I always say, business first."

"When I first got in, doing freestyles and

mixtapes, I did a song called "Still I Rise", I was talking about how so many women were pulling me down and ripping me apart. I said, 'Every time a door opens for me / That means you just got a better opportunity to do you / Better understand these labels look at numbers and statistics / If I win, you win, it's just logistics.'

"So in order for my theory to be proven right, I have to open

doors for women. The up-and-coming females who wanted to

get in—when you guys are coming out and dissing me, and all

that negativity....They saw me as a threat instead of seeing me as "she's going to open the door for us." I never came into what I'm doing dissing anyone.

I gave everyone their props and it's unfortunate that people felt intimidated and attacked me. Then it became a ripple effect. But now it's all love. My music is a way for me to have fun. Sometimes I'll say things and I'll laugh. But it's all love. I'm in a great place and I just wish everybody the best".

CHAPTER NINE
Time Marches Forward

In July of 2011, it was reported by The Dallas Observer that Nicki Minaj was arguing in a Dallas, Texas hotel with her, at the time, rumored boyfriend, Safaree Samuels. Here is what The Dallas Observer reported:

"Minaj and a 28-year-old black male by the name of Safaree Samuels were involved in an

argument at the Hotel Palomar's pool. Later, they returned to Nicki's room, where the two were staying together. There, the argument continued, at which point Samuels apparently decided

to leave, taking with him a suitcase that belonged to Nicki but that contained personal belongings of his. When Nicki protested, Samuels picked up the suitcase and "shoved it across [Nicki's] chin and lower lip."

"Samuels then left the scene and did not

return. At that point, a hotel employee called the police and fire department at Nicki's request, and, upon their arrival, Nicki was treated for bleeding on the inside of her lower lip. She declined to file charges against Samuels who has still not been found."

Prior to this incident, it was believed that Nicki Minaj was born in 1984, but due to the leaked police report from this incident, it became publicized that Nicki Minaj was born in 1982, and that she was a full two years older than a lot of people, including both many of her numerous fans within the general public as well as different media outlets.

Both Nicki Minaj and Safaree Samuels would go on to tweet about the situation on twitter.

Nicki Minaj would tweet:

"The fact that u believe a man either slapped or punched me in the face & didn't leave on a stretcher w/his balls hangin off? #getaF%cknLife"

Safaree Samuels tweeted:

**"The general public are some stupid muthafuckas!!!! Y'all dicks believe anything on a website....
It's really a shame... Wut up tho Dallas?!!"**

In September of 2012, Nicki Minaj became a judge for

the popular talent show, "American Idol". She joined RnB legend Mariah Carey, Keith Urban, and Randy Jackson. All of them were new, except for series staple, Randy Jackson. The very next month, in October, a video leaked and went viral, showing Nicki Minaj and Mariah Carey, in Charlotte, NC, arguing during auditions.

Mariah would go on to quote Nicki as saying:

"If I had a gun, I would shoot that bitch."

Nicki Minaj denies saying this.

Mariah would then say that Nicki's presence created an "unsafe work environment" and she beefed up her security.

Some people would say that they noticed tension between the two during episodes and Randy Jackson himself was later quoted as saying that "It was definitely difficult."

Nicki would go on to feud with Mariah via her twitter page.

Both Nicki Minaj and Mariah Carey would eventually leave the show, at the end of the season.

In the year of 2013, Nicki Minaj would go on to become the most charted female rap artist in the Billboard 100. She had 44 entries.

Nicki also became the very first person to win the BET Best Female Hip-Hop Artist Award four years in a row.

Nicki Minaj had plans to launch a record label called

"Pink Friday Records", but decided to drop that name, due to there being men on her label, saying that it wouldn't be fair to them. She signed Parker Ighile, Brinx, and possibly singer Keisha Renee and Blackout Movement.

During the spring of 2013, countless movies were being made. One of those movies, happened to star a woman named Cameron Diaz, a veteran actress. This film would also showcase another woman who is critically acclaimed in her own right, a woman who goes by the name of Nicki Minaj, in her first live action action film, "The Other Woman", in a small role. In "The Other Woman," Nicki played the role of Olivia's (played by Cameron Diaz) assistant, named "Lydia". The film also starred Leslie Mann and Kate Upton. Minaj has expressed a desire to continue acting, telling the Los Angeles Times:

"The movie thing —I definitely want to work at it more...I want to work on a character for my next role and take time out of my schedule to work on it — like sit there for a month and create someone. So yes, I want to do movies again. But am I gonna go tomorrow and start shooting? Probably not."

Although critically panned, "The Other Woman" went on to grab $196.7 million dollars at the box office, making a nice profit from it's $40 million dollar budget.

On May 21, 2014, Nicki Minaj released "Pills n Potions", the lead single to her upcoming album, "The Pinkprint". Later, during the Summer, she not only became the first music artist to get the BET Award for Best Hip Hop Artist five times in a row, but she also tied Hip Hop artist and legend Missy Elliot for having the most of that award.

She released the song and video for "Anaconda", the second single off of her album "The Pinkprint", in August of 2014, with it's whopping 19.6 million video views on it's first day on Vevo setting a 24 hour record on the popular website. The single became her highest charting U.S. single, peaking at the number two slot on the Billboard 100.

In November 2014, she released a lyric video to her song "Only", that had numerous people offended by what was considered "anti-Semitic" imagery.

The Anti Defamation League would be quoted as saying:

"...troubling that no one among Minaj's group of producers, publicists and managers raised a red flag about the use of such imagery before ushering the video into public release."

"insensitive to Holocaust survivors and a trivialization of the history of that era. The abuse of Nazi imagery is deeply disturbing and offensive to Jews and all those who can recall the

sacrifices **Americans and many others had to make as a result of Hitler's Nazi juggernaut."**

Nicki would take to twitter to discuss the situation:

"The artist who made the lyric video for 'Only' was influenced by a cartoon on Cartoon Network called *Metalocalypse* & *Sin City*...Both the producer, & person in charge of over seeing the lyric video (one of my best friends & videographer: A. Loucas), happen to be Jewish...I didn't come up w/the concept, but I'm very sorry & take full responsibility if it has offended anyone...I'd never condone Nazism in my art."

At the tail end of the year, Nicki Minaj was nominated for two Grammys: One for Best Rap Song and one for Best Pop Duo/Group Performance, for her single "Anaconda" and "Bang Bang" with Jessie J and Ariana Grande, respectively.

CHAPTER TEN

Love (The Sun Don't Shine Forever

In late 2014, Nicki Minaj and her boyfriend / former Hoodstar$ group mate / Hype man / rumored fiancee Safaree "SB" Samuels broke up, and even had a war of words on twitter. Safaree would go on Power 105's "The Breakfast Club" morning show, saying this about their breakup:

"I walked away. I'm not going to say I broke up, but I'm the one who walked away. I packed up my stuff and I left,"

"I just got to the point where the respect wasn't there," he continued. "Everyone around her works for her, you know? So it got the point where it was like, I'm your man. I'm who you go to sleep with every night. I'm who you wake up with every morning. And it got to the point where I was being treated like an employee, instead of like her man."

* * *

"I would never do anything publicly to try to pull her down. Whatever happens between me and her one on one is what it is, that's personal. I would never put that out there.

"I could be out here telling a million stories and doing cornball s--t, but I'm not gonna do that and I never plan on doing that. I just think it's crazy for her to come out now and try to pull me down and try to say I'm corny. I don't care who you with, who you with don't mean nothing to me. I want you to move on, because I'm moving on. I walked away from the situation."

On the rumors that Nicki is seeing Philadelphia Hip Hop artist Meek Mill:

"If that's who she decides to move on with, it is what it is. I'm not mad, I'm not bitter because if I wanted to make it work, I could've made it work... He don't owe me nothing. He's not the childhood friend I grew up with."

Nicki herself has denied being involved with Meek Mill in a romantic fashion.

Safaree also had this to add about the situation:

"Don't say, 'Oh, I don't have no talent' because every time it came to writing raps and doing music, it was me, her and a beat. She doesn't do it by herself. It was me and her. Don't discredit

me on what I've done for you, that's weak. I would never do that for her. All I'm saying is this is something me and her did together. That doesn't take away from what she's done. She's at the top of her league."

Several tracks on "The Pinkprint" are rumored to be about Safaree, though he says that he was there for the writing process of some of the album.

Nicki Minaj's "The Pinkprint" album is generally considered Nicki Minaj's best album to date. Rolling Stone listed it as the third best rap album of 2014. "The Pinkprint" sold 244,000 copies in it's first week, debuting at number two on the Billboard 200.

In October of 2014, Young Money Entertainment artist Tyga expressed his issues with the label via twitter, then went on to say this about his label mates, Drake and Nicki Minaj, while speaking with Vibe:

"I'm [trying to] go independent...I don't really get along with Drake."
"I don't like Drake as a person. He's just fake to me. I like his music, you know what I'm saying? I think his music is good, but we're all different people. We were forced together and it was kinda like we were forcing relationships together. It is what it is."

"I don't really get along with Nicki"

"I think being signed to Young Money, everybody felt like they had to force a relationship 'cause Wayne put us together...At the end of the day, the reason why I signed to Young Money is because of Wayne. Not because of Drake, not because of Nicki."

Shortly afterward, **Nicki unfollowed Tyga on Twitter.**

Birman, part owner of Cash Money Records, had this to say about the situation, while in a conversation with XXL:

"I always had respect for Tyga...We built something together. Another person we took from nothing to something. It will work itself out. It will work itself out. I'm just not with the Internet shit, saying nothing negative 'cause I can't say nothing negative about Tyga, 'cause I got respect for Tyga."

"I don't like him saying nothing negative about Drake and Nicki. To me, that shit ain't cool to me 'cause they never did no wrong to him. You understand me? But, he still the little homie and I do anything in the world for him. Nicki and Drake, that's the family. Whatever side you choose, it is what it is. But I ride with the team. I could say nothing bad about little Tyga. He's always been a man to me. A young man to me. A

69

young man to the team. This s**t coming out of left field to me. I don't understand it, but it is what it is."

In December of 2014, the unthinkable happened.

Lil Wayne announced that he wanted off of Cash Money Records, due to them not releasing his long awaited album, "The Carter V".

In January of 2015, TMZ reported that Lil Wayne was going to sue Birdman $51 million dollars and control of Young money Entertainment, taking control of the contracts of all of the artists that are on the Young Money Entertainment umbrella, including Drake and Nicki Minaj. What appears to make the situation even more complicated, is that Cash Money is the distributor of the artists on Young Money Entertainment, so the general consensus appears to be that the future of Young Money and Cash Money Empire will be very interesting, if nothing else.

CHAPTER ELEVEN
Epilogue

Nicki Minaj is a talented woman who has beaten the odds, possibly becoming more powerful than anyone in St. James, on that fateful Winter day of December 8, 1982, could have ever dreamed. Through all of her accomplishments, Nicki has persevered. It seems as if the latter half of 2014 may be a stressful time period, even for a woman who has been under pressure for years, and has only blown up as an international superstar. Nicki Minaj has proven herself to be a talented woman, defying the odds, and seems to have mastered her own destiny, or as close as any human possibly can. Only time will tell how Nicki Minaj, one of the most influential Hip Hop artists of all time, will further shape the words that will appear in life's story!

CHAPTER TWELVE

About The Author

About The Author

Valerie Mitchell was born on February 14, a day of love and celebration, to Wilson and Katherine Mitchell, Buffalo, NY.

Valerie now lives in Kansas City, with her husband Dale, two kids (with a third on the way!), and a spry little shitzu named Walmart (he was named after the owner of the parking lot he was found in!).

Printed in Great Britain
by Amazon

19663267R00047